SUBJECT		
Contents		

Understanding mental health

What does 'mental health' mean?

Mental health is the health of our mind.

It is about our thoughts, feelings and emotions as we live our lives every day.

Our mental health can affect how we feel, how we behave and the choices we make.

Everyone has mental health.

Mental = relating to the mind.

Our mind comes from inside our brain. It controls our thoughts, feelings, emotions and many other things to help our brain and body work.

Health = the condition of the human body.

Like our physical health (our bodies), there are things that can be healthy and unhealthy for our mental health (our minds).

What does 'wellbeing' mean?

Wellbeing means being comfortable, healthy and happy.

The link between **mental health** and **physical health**

Our minds and bodies are connected.

- **Keeping our bodies healthy helps to improve our mental health**
- **Keeping our minds healthy helps to improve our physical health**

What can help our mental and physical health?

- **Regular exercise**
- **Eating healthy foods**
- **Getting the right amounts of sleep**
- **Going to school and clubs**
- **Learning new subjects**
- **Reading books**
- **Spending time with friends and family**
- **Playing games**
- **Relaxing and having time to ourselves**
- **Visiting the doctors if we feel unwell**

What does being 'mentally healthy' mean?

If someone is '**mentally healthy**' or in '**good mental health**', they should be able to:

- **Feel happy and good about themselves most of the time**
- **Cope with day-to-day life and challenges**
- **Manage difficult feelings**
- **Take care of their physical health**
- **Get along well with friends and family**
- **Bounce back from tough times**
- **Make the most out of their potential**

What can affect our **mental health**?

Our mental health is affected by the things we do every day and the world around us - both good and bad.

Everyday things that can affect our mental health include:

- **How much sleep we get**
- **How often we exercise**
- **The people around us**
- **Making big decisions**
- **Coping with change**

- **School and education**
- **What we eat and drink**
- **Our surroundings**
- **World events, such as the coronavirus pandemic**

Let's look at some examples:

Exercise

Not only does regular exercise build our physical strength, but it also helps to build our mental strength.

Not exercising enough can increase the risk of developing physical health problems, leading to mental health problems.

Sleep

A good night's sleep makes us feel alert, gives us energy and helps us to concentrate better.

Not getting enough sleep can make us feel tired, exhausted and makes it harder to focus.

These examples show us that everyday things can affect our mental health in good and bad ways, and everyone is affected differently.

Emotions and feelings

The words 'emotions' and 'feelings' are very similar, but they have different meanings.

Emotions

Emotions happen in response to an event or situation.

For example, we may experience 'happiness' when we are having fun with our friends.

Emotions come from inside our brain but can affect our whole body and the way we feel.

Events or situations trigger our emotions.

Feelings

Feelings are the way we feel in our minds and bodies as we process our emotions.

For example, the happiness we experience having fun with our friends can make us feel excited.

Emotions trigger our feelings.

Recognising **emotions** and **feelings**

Emotions and feelings are an important part of our lives. It is helpful to understand how to name and recognise them.

Emotions and feelings can be described using words, facial expressions and body language.

Let's explore five types of emotion and find out how we may feel after experiencing each of them.

	Emotion	Feeling...
	Happiness	Happy, calm, relaxed, excited, joyful.
	Sadness	Sad, unhappy, upset, lonely, disappointed.
	Fear	Worried, scared, anxious, nervous, frightened.
	Surprise	Surprised, excited, shocked, alarmed, stunned.
	Anger	Angry, stressed, frustrated, unhappy, annoyed.

Some emotions make us feel happy, whereas some emotions create difficult feelings, like feeling frightened.

The important thing to remember is that all emotions are a normal part of being human.

Why should we express our feelings?

Expressing how we feel is good for our mental health.

It can help us to feel:

- **Supported**
- **Positive**
- **Less stressed**
- **Confident**
- **Understood**
- **Less worried**

How emotions and feelings change our behaviour

Our emotions and feelings can impact our behaviour in good and bad ways.

For example, an emotion such as 'happiness' may improve our behaviour because it 'sharpens' our senses, makes us feel good and give us motivation.

On the other hand, an emotion like 'anger' can stop us from making good decisions and make us behave in a way that we may regret once the feelings have passed.

Mental health mood scale

Our mental health, including our emotions and feelings, can be thought of as being on a scale.

Our mental health can move along the scale depending on how we feel and what is happening around us.

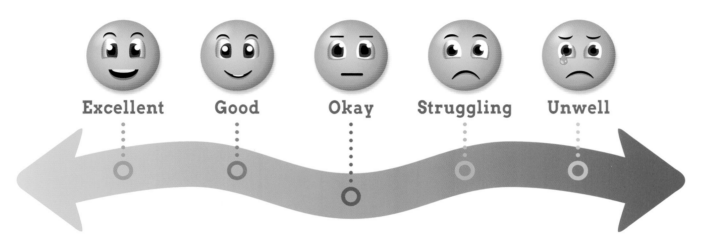

Excellent   Good   Okay   Struggling   Unwell

Most of the time, our mental health will move between the "Excellent" and "Okay" areas as we live every day.

Every so often, we may move into the "Struggling" area due to things happening in our lives, which is normal.

However, sometimes our mental health can move in and out of the "Unwell" area or stay there for a long time.

This is not so good for our mental health or physical health and can put a huge strain on our daily lives.

The good news is that wherever we are on the scale, there are things we can do to look after our mental health and stay healthy.

See pages 26-28 to find out how we can look after our mental health.

Mixed emotions

Not only do we experience different emotions, but we can also experience different emotions at the same time.

This is known as "mixed emotions" or "conflicting emotions" and is very common.

For example, we can feel both happy and sad, or nervous but excited at the same time.

It is important to understand that it is okay to feel a mix of emotions, even if it is not a nice feeling.

Experiencing feelings such as fear or jealousy can help us learn about ourselves and the people around us.

Examples:

Feeling **happy** after revising well for a school test.

Feeling **nervous** about achieving the pass mark.

Feeling **disappointed** about our favourite sports team losing a game.

Feeling **proud** because they tried their very best to win the game.

Mental health problems

Everyone experiences mental health problems at some point in their life.

For most people, mental health problems do not last very long and happen because of a life event, such as the death of a family member or falling out with friends for a long time.

Some people, who have had their mental health problem recognised by a doctor, may have thoughts, feelings and emotions that affect their everyday lives, or that come and go at different stages in their lives.

In most cases, we can recognise and treat mental health problems using self-help, talking therapy and medication.

Self-help: Things we can do to help ourselves feel better.

Talking therapy: A way of treating mental health problems by talking to a therapist or doctor.

Medication: Medicine, such as tablets to ease the symptoms of mental health problems.

What causes mental health problems?

There is no single cause of mental health problems.

It is usually lots of different things that make someone more likely to develop a mental health problem.

Some people might be more affected by these things than others, as everyone is different.

Some examples include:

- Genes (DNA) inherited from family members

- Experiencing pain or suffering

- The death of a relative or friend

- Long-term stress

- Physical health problems

- Loneliness

- Being bullied or mistreated

- Money problems

Signs of a
mental health problem

It can be challenging to identify someone who is suffering from a mental health problem.

Possible signs may include:

- Low mood, feeling upset and tearful

- Losing interest in activities and hobbies

- Not doing as well at school with no clear reason

- Feeling tired and exhausted most of the time

- Not wanting to be with friends and family

- Changes in eating and drinking, such as skipping meals

- Changes in awareness such as hearing or seeing things that others do not

- Troubled sleep patterns – not getting enough sleep or sleeping too much

The impact of
mental health problems

Day-to-day: Mental health problems can make it harder for people to cope with day-to-day activities.

Physical health: Mental health problems can affect people's ability to protect and develop their physical health.

Education: Learning can be more difficult when living with a mental health problem, stopping students from being all they can be.

Hobbies and clubs: Poor mental health can result in a loss of interest in hobbies and clubs that are a large part of a person's life.

Family and friends: Mental health problems can affect relationships, leading to people not wanting to be with family and friends.

Loneliness

What is loneliness?

Loneliness is when we feel sad or distressed due to being alone when we don't want to be.

It is also possible to feel lonely when we are with other people, such as our friends or family.

Social isolation, where we are separated from other people, is different to loneliness.

Although, long periods of social isolation can lead to loneliness.

Being socially isolated can occur because of life events, such as being poorly or injured or being told to stay at home due to the coronavirus pandemic.

Possible causes of loneliness

There are lots of reasons why we may feel lonely and it can affect everyone differently.

- **Being apart from other people**
- **Finding it hard to make friends or being left out of a group**
- **Problems communicating with other people**
- **Having a disability or illness**
- **Moving to a new area**
- **Moving schools**
- **Being bullied**
- **Losing a close friend, relative or family pet**
- **Mental health problems**

Ways to cope with
Loneliness

- Talk about how we feel to a trusted adult or close friend

- Join a group or club that focuses on something we enjoy and make it part of our weekly routine

- Visit places where we can be around other people, such as going to the park or visiting the cinema

- Make changes to our lifestyle to help us feel more in control and feel good about ourselves

- We can try peer support, where people use their experiences to help other people who are facing similar challenges

- Lots of mental health charities offer peer support online and in person, such as the mental health charity Mind **www.mind.org.uk**

- We could also phone a mental health charity if we need to talk to someone in private

Childline
Telephone: 0800 1111
Website: www.childline.org.uk

Samaritans
Telephone: 116 123
Website: www.samaritans.org

Stress

What is **stress**?

Stress is a feeling we get when we feel under pressure to do something.

It is the way our bodies respond to challenges or difficult things.

A small challenge gets us ready for action and motivates us to get things done.

But too big of a challenge can affect our thoughts, feelings and stop us from enjoying life.

Causes of **stress**

Lots of things can cause stress and it affects people differently. When we know what is causing our stress, it can be easier to find ways to cope with it.

Possible causes of **stress**

- **School, homework and exams**
- **Having too many things to do**
- **Being unprepared for something**
- **Big life changes, like moving house or schools**
- **Relationship problems with friends and family**
- **Having an illness or injury**
- **Being bullied**
- **Loneliness**
- **Lack of sleep**

Ways to cope with Stress

- Talk about how we feel to a close friend or trusted adult

- Plan ahead for busy days – make a list of things we need to remember

- Try not to leave things until the last minute, like homework or exam revision. Get things done as soon as you can

- If we are finding it hard to start a task, we can break it down into smaller parts and tackle one part at a time

- Exercise is a good stress reliever. It will not make stress disappear, but it helps us to clear our thoughts and to deal with things more calmly

- Have time for ourselves. We could go for a walk, read a book, listen to our favourite music or have a relaxing bath

- Get enough sleep. A good sleep routine is important to stop us from getting too stressed. The better rested we are, the better we can cope with pressure

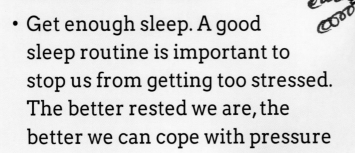

Feeling **unhappy**

It is normal to feel unhappy from time to time, but for some people, their feelings of unhappiness affect how they think, feel and behave every day.

When a person feels down or unhappy for a long time and they find it hard to control their feelings, they should see a doctor who can help them.

Not only do doctors and nurses help us with physical health problems, like when we get injured, but they also help us with mental health problems.

The doctor will run some tests and ask the person some questions to find out what is causing their feelings of unhappiness.

They may explain things that the person can do for themselves to help them feel better.

However, if their feelings of unhappiness last for a long time, their doctor may identify the problem as a condition called 'depression'.

Depression

Depression is a common mental health problem that can affect people of all ages.

Depression is more than simply feeling unhappy for a few days. When someone is depressed, they feel unhappy for weeks or months, rather than just a few days.

The good news is that with the right support, it is possible to treat depression.

Feeling worried

Feeling worried is normal, and we all experience feelings of worry.

For example, we may feel worried about sitting an exam or auditioning for the school play. During times like this, feeling worried is normal.

However, some people find it hard to control their feelings of worry.

Their feelings last a long time and are much more intense.

They may worry about things that other people do not worry about at all.

When people feel worried like this, they should see a doctor to find out more about their feelings and identify the causes.

In some cases, where worry affects a person for several weeks, the doctor may identify the problem as a condition called 'anxiety'.

Anxiety

Like depression, anxiety is a common mental health problem that can affect people of all ages..

Anxiety can be described as uncontrollable feelings of worry, nervousness or unease about many different things in everyday life.

Although anxiety can affect people's daily lives, treatments are available to ease their worries and help them feel better.

Anxiety vs. feeling anxious
Depression vs. feeling depressed

What is the difference?

The words 'depressed' and 'anxious' can be used in conversation to describe how someone feels.

But this does not always mean they have been told by a doctor that they have depression or anxiety.

Both depression (unhappiness) and anxiety (worry) can be experienced by people with or without a doctor knowing what is happening to them.

The difference between just 'feeling anxious or depressed' from time to time and the mental health conditions depression and anxiety, comes from the strength of someone's feelings and how long those feelings last.

We cannot always see mental health problems, but they are just as important as physical health problems.

Unlike physical health problems, where we can often see what is wrong with a person, we cannot always see mental health problems from outside the body.

Mental health problems do create physical symptoms, but most symptoms occur inside our bodies.

Remember, just because we cannot see the symptoms, it does not mean they are not as important.

Mental health problems are equally important to physical health problems and there should not be any shame in getting help.

Professional help is available to anyone who may need it, both children and adults.

OUR MENTAL HEALTH IS IMPORTANT

Talking about mental health

Sometimes it helps to talk to someone about our feelings, but it can be hard to find the right person and know what to say to them.

However, a simple conversation can start to make things better.

It is okay to ask for help.

Whenever our feelings are getting too big to cope with on our own and they affect our daily lives, talking to someone we trust can really help.

Think about what we do when we are feeling sick or we hurt ourselves. What do we do?

We will probably tell someone we know and go and get it checked by a doctor.

Like our physical health problems, we need to treat our mental health problems in the same way.

Speaking to someone we trust can help us stay mentally healthy and stop our mental health problems from getting any worse.

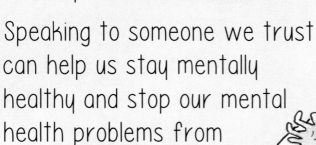

How to talk about mental health

Step 1 Make a plan

Making a plan about what we want to say can help organise our thoughts and prompt us if we forget what we are going to say.

Here are some ideas for making a plan:

- **Write down some questions we need answers to**
- **Gather information from trusted sources online that might help explain what we are feeling** (see page 30 for some trusted websites)
- **Write down a list of feelings, emotions or behaviours we are experiencing**
- **Choose a time where we feel most comfortable**

Step 2 Decide who to talk to

We can start by picking people we trust and those who will listen to what we have to say.

Sharing our feelings with a close friend is a good starting point as they should be supportive.

However, our friends will have limited ways to help compared to a trusted adult, so we will also need to talk to a trusted adult.

Some of the people we could speak to may include:

- **Parent, carer or close relative**
- **Teacher or teaching assistant**
- **A school nurse or school counsellor**
- **Other members of staff in school**
- **Club leader or sports coach**
- **Mental health charities, such as Childline or Samaritans**

Step 3 Start the conversation

We may feel nervous about starting the conversation, but once we have spoken to the right person, it should help our situation.

Here are some tips:

- **Use our written plan to remind us of what to say**

- **Make sure we are in the right place without interruptions**

- **Ask them if we can share something with them**

- **Tell the person how we are feeling in an open and honest way**

- **Do not rush the conversation, we should go at our own pace**

- **We do not have to share everything at once. If the person responds in a good way, we can always talk to them again**

Listening to other people's
worries

If someone wants to share their concerns with us, we do not need to know all the answers.

Sometimes it is best to listen, be supportive and encourage them to speak to a trusted adult.

Here are some tips:

- **Listen to them carefully**
- **Do not interrupt when they are speaking**
- **Show an interest in what the person is saying**
- **Do not judge the person**
- **Recognise the courage it has taken for them to talk**
- **Encourage them to talk to a trusted adult**
- **Do not tell them what you think is wrong with them**

Talking about mental health can take time, and it often takes more than one conversation for people to seek further help.

However, there are situations where we should get help right away.

> **We should tell a trusted adult immediately if someone is in any kind of danger.**

Looking after our mental health

Looking after our mental health is just as important as keeping physically healthy.

Here are some tips on how we can look after our mental health.

1- Talk about our feelings

Talking to people we trust about how we feel and asking for help is good for our mental health. Likewise, if we open up about our own feelings, it might encourage others to do the same.

2 - Exercise regularly

As we have discovered, our bodies and minds are connected. When we take care of our physical health, we also take care of our mental health and the other way around.

Exercise can:

- **Keep us healthy**
- **Lift our mood**
- **Boost our energy levels**
- **Build our confidence**
- **Help us sleep better**
- **Help us feel better**

3 - Eat a balanced diet

Food is our fuel. It gives us essential nutrients that help our bodies work, including our brains. The better we eat, the better we will function.

A balanced diet rich in nutrients, including fruit and vegetables, helps protect our mental health.

4 - Get enough sleep

Getting enough sleep plays an important role in good mental and physical health.

Not getting enough sleep can leave us feeling tired and exhausted.

When we get the right amount of sleep, we feel more alert, less tense and concentrate better.

The amount of sleep we need depends on our bodies and age.

We should know that we are getting enough sleep when we do not feel sleepy during the day.

5 - Keep in touch

Keeping in touch with our friends and family is important for our mental health.

Not only can friends and family make us feel supported and less lonely, but they can also give us advice when we need help.

6 - Do something we enjoy

Doing something we enjoy can make us feel good about ourselves.

Hobbies and activities can relieve tension, give us a sense of achievement and help us forget about our worries.

Trying something new can also help our mental health. We may discover talents that we never knew we had!

Other activities that support mental health

- **Reading books or listening to audiobooks**
- **Listening to music**
  - **Learning new skills**
  - **Spending time outdoors**
  - **Hobbies and clubs**
  - **Volunteering**
  - **Relaxing and having time for ourselves**
- **Arts and crafts**
- **Playing games with friends**

Looking out for other people

When someone has a mental health problem, they can often lose touch with their friends and family.

This is because they struggle to cope and do not think people will understand what they are going through.

It is important to look out for the people around us. Our support and understanding could play a part in helping them overcome their problem.

Tips for looking out for others

- **Be there for them during tough times. It does not have to be in person. We could call them or speak to them online**

- **Do helpful things to get them through the day. Even the smallest acts of kindness can help. Hold the door open for them in the corridor, eat lunch together, discuss schoolwork or help to carry their bags**

- **Learn more about mental health to get a better understanding of what they are experiencing. We may find things that we can do to help them feel better**

- **Encourage them to talk to a trusted adult if they have not done so already**

- **Show an interest in their opinions, cultures and beliefs**

- **Speak to a trusted adult if we are worried about someone and do not know what to do next**

Further information

Here are some useful websites to learn more about mental health.

National Health Service (NHS)

The NHS provides health care for all people in the UK. Their website includes lots of information on mental health, including the signs and treatments of mental health problems and self-help advice.

Website: www.nhs.uk/mental-health

Young Minds

Young Minds has lots of practical tips and advice from young people themselves and information on getting support.

Website: www.youngminds.org.uk

Mind

Mind provides advice and support to empower anyone experiencing a mental health problem. The Mind website has a helpful 'A to Z' directory of mental health topics to explore.

Website: www.mind.org.uk

Mental health support

These services offer free, private support from trained volunteers. We can talk about anything that is troubling us and we do not have to give out our names.

Childline

We can talk to Childline about anything. No problem is too big or too small.

Call: 0800 1111
Website: www.childline.org.uk

Samaritans

We can talk to Samaritans for free, from any phone, day and night.

Call: 116 123
Website: www.samaritans.org

Shout

We can send Shout a text and we should receive a reply in as little as 5 minutes.

Text: "SHOUT" to 85258
Website: www.giveusashout.org

Keywords

Affect: To create a change in someone or something.

Anxiety: Strong feelings of worry that last a long time.

Depression: Strong feelings of unhappiness that last a long time.

Emotions: Mental reactions caused by events or situations, resulting in changes to the body and mind.

Experience: An event or situation that leaves an impression on someone.

Feelings: The physical and mental sensations we feel as we process our emotions.

Health: The overall condition of the human body.

Loneliness: Feelings of sadness or distress due to being alone when we don't want to be.